THE ALCHEMY OF GRIEF

poems

EMILY FERRARA

∞

ALCHIMIA DEL DOLORE

traduzione

SABINE PASCARELLI

BORDIGHERA PRESS

Library of Congress Control Number: 2007938304

Cover Photo: © Judith M. Daniels
Cover Design: © Deborah S. Starewich and Judith M. Daniels

The Bordighera Poetry Prize
is made possible by a generous grant from
The Sonia Raiziss-Giop Charitable Foundation.

Printed in the United States.

Published by
BORDIGHERA PRESS
John D. Calandra Italian American Institute
25 W. 43rd Street, 17th Floor
New York, NY 10036

BORDIGHERA POETRY PRIZE 9
ISBN 1-884419-89-5 (softcover)
ISBN 1-884419-90-9 (hardcover)

Acknowledgments

I am grateful to the editors of the following publications in which the following poems previously appeared:

Ballard Street Poetry Journal, "Women in a Hot Tub"
Family Medicine, "Bad News in the ER"
Full Circle Journal, "Poem for Jack Spicer, Deadbeat Poet"
Lifeboat: A Journal of Memoir, "Frogs"
Lumina, "The Difference"
Lynx Eye, "Rapture"
Rough Places Plain: Poems of the Mountains,
    "The Highest Places"
VIA, "Mother's Lament," "Afterbirth," "The Winter After,"
    "Succulence," "Alchemy," "Redemption at Sea," "Aubade"
Worcester Review, "The Winter After"

My deepest thanks to Barbara Helfgott Hyett and the members of "Poem Works: The Workshop for Publishing Poets" in Brookline, Massachusetts, and Newfoundland, Canada, for guidance, inspiration and support in the making of these poems. Thanks also to Leigh Emery, Mary Jo Moore, Linda Warren, and Susan Roney O'Brien who provided invaluable feedback on the manuscript. I am grateful for writing sanctuary provided in Vermont by Holly Robinson Cookson; in Provincetown by Brad Drabant and Michael Cronin; and in Maine, by the generosity of colleagues at UMass Medical School and the Greenfire Retreat Center. I am indebted to the following teachers who honed my foundational writing skills to prepare me: Lael Wertenbaker, Gerald Powers, Virginia Gunter, Judith Beth Cohen, and Mary Clare Powell.

I wish to acknowledge the writing of Kat Duff whose essay "The Alchemy of Illness" (in her book of the same name [Pantheon, 1993]) inspired the scaffolding for this collection of poems, as well as source material by C.G. Jung on alchemy and the psyche.

And finally, I am grateful to all of my friends and family who have provided loving support, especially my parents Ray and Nancy Ferrara; M. Lara Hoke, my life partner and steadfast anchor; and Deva Jasheway, my daughter, whose vibrance and depth are a beacon.

in memory of my son

ADAM FERRARA JASHEWAY

1984–2003

in memoria di mio figlio

ADAM FERRARA JASHEWAY

1984–2003

CONTENTS

INDICE

"Death has nothing to do with going away."
— Rumi, *Ode 911*; trans. Coleman Barks

"La morte non ha nulla a che fare con l'andar via."

— Rumi, *Ode 911*; trad. Coleman Barks

I. Calcinatio

SLOW BURN

I gaze at the hot coals.
Take fire into my marrow.
Watch the life I knew melt
at my feet. Stomp the past.
Pass through pools of regret.
Feel blood rush hot and fast
through my breast.
Become the flames.
Consume you.

BRUCIARE LENTAMENTE

Fissare i carboni ardenti.
Prendere fuoco nel mio midollo.
Guardare la vita che conoscevo dissolta
ai miei piedi. Pestare il passato.
Attraversare stagni di rimpianti.
Sentire il sangue scorrere caldo e veloce
nel mio petto.
Diventare fiamme.
Consumarti.

MOTHER'S LAMENT

Your feet tagged,
tinged blue, hang
over the gurney's edge.
Head thrust back,
mouth slack,
hands folded cold
turning colder.
I reach for life
in your muscled body,
carefully sheathed.
Your cropped hair still
grows warm. I murmur,
touch your head, place
my mouth to your cheek.
Wrench free the taut sheet.
See your penis at rest:
crimson, pure, your blood rushed
all your lean pubescence to ripen there.
I want to cast out the affront
of the yellow catheter
still inserted in you.
All I want is your flesh,
slick and warm as the day
you were born.

LAMENTO DI MADRE

I tuoi piedi etichettati,
blu venati, pendono
dal bordo della lettiga.
Testa ripiegata,
bocca allentata,
mani incrociate fredde
sempre più fredde.
Cerco di afferrare la vita
dal tuo corpo muscoloso,
accuratamente fasciato.
I tuoi capelli tosati ancora
caldi. Sussurro,
ti tocco la testa, porto
la bocca alla tua guancia.
Strappo via il lenzuolo teso.
Vedo il tuo pene a riposo:
rossastro, puro, là il tuo sangue riversò
a maturare la tua magra pubescenza.
Vorrei tirar via l'insulto
del giallo catetere
ancora inserito.
Tutto ciò che voglio è la tua carne,
liscia e calda come il giorno
in cui sei nato.

ADAM SPEAKS

first   father came and sat with me   quiet, communing
then sister glimpsed my corpse   head thrown back in death
like a narwhal   jaw jutting   gasp   mother called
my name   touched my hair   forehead   cheek   the blessing
of her warmth   my heart quiet in my chest   and hers
beating furiously   to catch up with me

ADAM PARLA

prima   padre giunse e sedette con me   tranquillo, raccolto
poi sorella dette uno sguardo rapido alla mia salma   alla mia
testa ricadente nella morte   come un narvalo   mandibola
sporgente   boccheggiando   madre chiamò il mio nome
toccò i miei capelli   la fronte   la guancia   la benedizione del
suo calore   il mio cuore tranquillo nel petto   ed il suo
battendo furiosamente   per raggiungermi

BAD NEWS IN THE ER

The serious young doctor
started the story
at the beginning.

"Your son was at a concert
when he collapsed."
Can I see him?
"An ambulance was called.
EMTs started CPR."
Where is he?
"They tried to revive him,
but got no response."
Please...
"They brought him here.
We worked a long time."
Oh God.
"We didn't want to give up.
He was so young."

I searched the doctor for sorrow
found a stoic earnestness.
He ended with an apology.

"I'm so sorry," he said,
as if he'd hurt my feelings,
as if I could forgive him.

BRUTTE NOTIZIE NELL'ER[1]

Il serio, giovane medico
cominciò la storia
dall'inizio.

"Suo figlio era al concerto
quando si accasciò."
Posso vederlo?
"Fu chiamata un'ambulanza.
Gli EMT[2] fecero una CPR[3]."
Dov'è?
"Cercarono di rianimarlo,
ma non ci fu reazione."
Per favore...
"Lo portarono qui.
Lavorammo a lungo."
Oh Dio.
"Non volevamo arrenderci.
Era così giovane."

Cercai di scoprire dolore nel medico,
trovai una serietà impassibile.
Concluse con delle scuse.

"Mi dispiace tanto", disse,
come se avesse offeso i miei sentimenti,
come se gli potessi perdonare.

---

[1]*Emergency Room*; Sala Rianimazione.
[2]*Emergency Medical Technician*; Medici del 118.
[3]*Cardiopulmonary Resuscitation*; Rianimazione Cardiopolmonare.

EATING BORSCHT AT CAFÉ ST. PETERSBURG

The cream curdles atop
blood-dark liquid, hunks
of gristled meat clot
my gums, congeal,
hateful on my tongue. Fractured
art struts the wall: a beak, a breast,
a zipper, an ass,
no eyes. I am lost
in brilliance draped green.
Observe me, fringed and jarred,
undone.

MANGIANDO BORSCHT AL CAFÉ ST. PETERSBURG

La crema caglia sopra
del liquido come sangue scuro, grossi tocchi
di carne cartilaginosa s'incollano
alle mie gengive, si raggrumano
odiosi sulla lingua. Frammenti
d'arte imbrattano il muro: un becco, un seno,
una cerniera, un sedere,
niente occhi. Sono perduta
in una luminosità drappeggiata verde.
Osservami, sfrangiata e scossa,
disfatta.

IN FIGUERES

After Dali

Once I had a nodding acquaintance
with disaster. Monstrous eggs danced
the crest of a tower. Loaves
of bread, crusty and golden, climbed
a well-crafted moustache. Blossoms
turned inward on themselves. The sky
withered as lightning bugs dimmed
against purple-black. Now I measure
the curve of each day by my penchant
for meeting another's gaze: imploring,
dazed, blank or piercing. I face
the mirror, seek increments.
The elastic afternoon bends.

In Figueres

Secondo Dali

Una volta sfiorai il disastro.
Uova mostruose danzarono
sulla cresta di una torre. Filoni di
pane, croccanti e dorati, assalirono
dei baffi ben fatti. Fiori
si richiusero in se stessi. Il cielo appassì
e le lucciole si affievolirono contro
il nero-porpora. Adesso misuro la curva
di ogni giorno dalla mia indole per incontrare
lo sguardo di un altro: implorante, allucinato,
inespressivo o penetrante. Mi rivolgo
verso lo specchio, cerco sviluppi.
L'elastico pomeriggio s'inarca.

THE HEALER

She places cones of moxa
on ten points plotted
across my back. These
she lights from left to right.
When my skin is seared, coal
threatening to scar, only now
do I feel. Cool salve
on my skin. Quick prick
of needle to release
stagnant energy,
my unrequited grief.

LA GUARITRICE

Appoggia coni di moxa[1]
nei dieci punti segnati
sulla mia schiena.
Li accende da sinistra a destra.
Quando la mia pelle è bruciacchiata, carbone
che minaccia di lasciare cicatrici, solo allora
sento. Fresca pomata
sulla mia pelle. Veloce puntura
d'ago per liberare
energia stagnante,
il mio dolore senza vendetta.

[1]candele di artemisia usate in agopuntura.

II. SOLUTIO

ON THE FIFTH DAY

At the funeral home
they brought you to us
for the final viewing.

You were even colder,
and as beautiful as
I remembered. I knew

time had passed because
stubble broke through
the skin of your jaw

shaved smooth
hours before death.
I thought you might sit up.

Shudder. Roll over. Didn't I
see you breathe, your chest rise
ever so slightly?

The pastor prayed over you,
clipped wisps of your hair, took
your photograph.

IL QUINTO GIORNO

L'impresa delle pompe funebri
ti portò da noi
per l'ultimo sguardo.

Eri ancora più freddo
e così bello come
ti ricordavo. Sapevo

che era passato del tempo per
i peli di barba fuorusciti dalla
pelle del tuo mento

rasato liscio
alcune ore prima della tua morte.
Pensai che potevi metterti a sedere.

Fremere. Girarti. Non ti
vedevo forse respirare, il tuo petto alzarsi
anche lievemente?

Il pastore pregò sopra di te,
tagliò delle ciocche dai tuoi capelli, prese
la tua fotografia.

SUBMERGED

the literal dissolution

    tears rain
        tears rain
            tears rain

limitless
motherless

    tears rain
        tears rain
            tears rain

indelible
oneness

    tears rain
        tears rain
            tears rain

the purity and solidity of snow

SOMMERSA

Il vero e proprio scioglimento

    lacrime pioggia
        lacrime pioggia
            lacrime pioggia

senza limiti
senza madre

    lacrime pioggia
        lacrime pioggia
            lacrime pioggia

incancellabile
unità

    lacrime pioggia
        lacrime pioggia
            lacrime pioggia

la purezza e la solidità della neve

THE CURE

You flew home at the
lunar eclipse, your heart
in repose
finally perfect, finally
cured. No more

valve gone awry, aortic root
overblown, unbeknownst
to medicine and my careful
vigilance. There is nowhere

to hide from
your absence. I drown
in spaciousness.

LA GUARIGIONE

Volasti a casa per
l'eclissi lunare, il tuo cuore
a riposo
finalmente perfetto, finalmente
risanato. Niente più

valvola malandata, diramazione aortica
dilatata, non riconosciuta
dalla medicina e la mia attenta
vigilanza. Non c'è luogo

per nascondermi alla
tua assenza. Quasi annegassi
nello spazio.

CREMATION

I.
The man who tended you wore gloves.
He did not pray. He worked the rake
through your remains, then swept
the chamber of your nakedness,
ground to seven pounds of pale
bone and ash in a wooden urn.

II.
Under a swatch of blue I scavenge
for you: gulls plunder
an empty lifeguard chair,
whitecaps rush the shore.
Every beach brims with sorrow
and kindnesses. Brims with you.

CREMAZIONE

I.
L'uomo che si occupò di te indossò dei guanti.
Non pregò. Rovistò con il rastrello
fra le tue spoglie, poi spazzò
la stanza dalla tua nudità,
ridotta a sette libbra di pallide
ossa e ceneri in un'urna di legno.

II.
Sotto un lembo di cielo blu disperatamente
ti cerco: alcuni gabbiani saccheggiano
una vecchia seggiola da bagnino,
onde spumeggianti si riversano sulla costa.
Ogni spiaggia trabocca di dolore
e gentilezze. Trabocca di te.

AFTERBIRTH

Let me not
make a talisman
of your eyelashes
nor your ashes
nor bones delivered
from the fire.
Slow, deep, my
muscles sighing
in the progression
of algebra, my os
briny as sealskin,
my waters breaking
below the blossom
of your head.
Let me place you
in the seedbed
of my body.

PLACENTA

Non farò
un talismano delle tue ciglia
né delle tue ceneri
né delle ossa salvate
dal fuoco.
Piano, profondamente, i miei
muscoli sospirano
come nella progressione
dell'algebra, la mia os
salata come pelle di foca,
le mie acque si rompono
sotto il fiore
della tua testa.
Lascia che ti posi
nel semenzaio
del mio corpo.

THE WINTER AFTER

Sitting in my room before sunrise
I clasp my breath. Since yesterday
snow has been falling, hushed,
measurable in feet. By my bed
the window screen fills with snow.
I am blind to the lake below,
its ashen face, its brokenness.
I am lashed to icefields.
Unseen geese bleed
through this gauze, dispassionate.
They fill the air with howling.
What does it matter?
This is not their story.

I made an altar in his room.
The ceramic Buddha, muted
gold and taupe, holds
his guitar pick in a cupped palm.
The figure is draped with two cloths,
gifts friends gave me at the funeral:
a red and ochre prayer scarf,
a hundred-year-old handkerchief to hold
the grief of a mother for her son.

I go to his room, bow down
to my penance, open
the bureau drawer, choose a sweater—
today olive green trimmed gray.
"You never wear your own clothes anymore"
says my daughter, wondering
what's become of her mother.

L'Inverno Dopo

Seduta all'alba nella mia camera
trattengo il respiro. Da ieri
la neve cade, silenziosa,
crescendo velocemente. Vicino al mio letto
la retina alla finestra si riempie di neve.
Ignoro il lago laggiù,
la sua faccia cinerea, le sue spaccature.
Sono legata alle sue lastre di ghiaccio.
Il richiamo di invisibili oche, spassionate,
passa come sangue da questa garza.
Esse riempiono d'ululato l'aria.
Che importa?
Questa non è la loro storia.

Ho eretto un altare nella sua stanza.
Il Buddha di ceramica, di oro
spento brunastro, ha il suo plettro
di chitarra nel palmo socchiuso.
La statuetta è drappeggiata con due tessuti,
doni di amici ricevuti al funerale:
rosso-ocra lo scialle da preghiera e ancora, il
fazzoletto vecchio cent'anni per contenere
il dolore di una madre per il figlio.

Vado nella sua stanza, mi inchino
alla mia penitenza, apro
il cassetto, scelgo un maglione—
oggi verde oliva bordato di grigio.
"Non stai portando più i tuoi vestiti"
dice mia figlia, chiedendosi
che n'è divenuto di sua madre.

III. Sublimatio

RAPTURE

Devoted to studying
the night sky, I peer
through a telescope, find
the comet's tail.
I try to see eternity, each star
a point of entry. I am translator
of space and time.
Do you hear?

ESTASI

Devota a studiare
il cielo notturno, scruto
attraverso un telescopio, trovo
la coda della cometa.
Cerco di vedere l'eternità, ogni stella
un punto d'entrata. Sono traduttrice
di spazio e tempo.
Senti?

Sunday Afternoon with My Children

We hiked to a clearing
under a refuge of pines

come silence, come care,
to the church of my longing

We lay on a bed of pine needles,
thick as eiderdown, and as soft,
our legs splayed
in a six-pointed star.

come silence, come care

The trinity
of our voices chanting
laughter, rare song
no longer possible.

come silence

DOMENICA POMERIGGIO CON I MIEI FIGLI

Scarpiniamo fino ad una radura
sotto un rifugio di pini

vieni silenzio, vieni premura,
alla chiesa del mio desiderio

Sdraiati su un letto di aghi di pino,
spesso e morbido come piuma,
le nostre gambe allargate
a formare una stella a sei punte.

vieni silenzio, vieni premura

La trinità delle nostre voci che cantano,
risata, raro canto
non più possibile.

vieni silenzio

In Absentia

"We're constantly mistaking ourselves for something eternal."
  — René Daumal, *Mount Analogue,* trans. Roger Shattuck

Where death and life are
indistinct, everything exists
at once. Tidal rivers
moan under the weight
of melting, the hollowed
trunks of wind, God
groaning, the moon
one day short of full.
Rumi tells me
death has nothing to do
with going away
but I know he is wrong.

In Absentia

"Costantemente sbagliamo a prenderci per qualcosa di eterno."
— René Daumal, *Mount Analogue,* trad. Roger Shattuck

Dove morte e vita sono
indistinte, ogni cosa esiste
contemporaneamente. Fiumi in piena
si lamentano sotto il peso
dello scioglimento, gli incavati
tronchi del vento, Dio
che geme, la luna
un giorno prima d'essere piena.
Rumi mi dice
la morte non ha nulla a che fare
con l'andar via
ma io so che sbaglia.

SUCCULENCE

Saguaro is my sustenance,
offers red-pulped fruit to fox and ant,
shelters gilded flickers, gila woodpeckers,
holds rain in pleated reservoirs
to feed a month of blossoms
in spring. The joy is unremitting,
ephemeral: a nightly spectacle
of luminosity, perished
in the heat of next day's sun.
Of such use is even short-lived succulence.

SUCCULENZA

Il Saguaro[1] è il mio sostentamento,
offre polpa rossa a volpe e formica,
da riparo ai *flicker* dorati, ai picchi *gila*[2],
conserva la pioggia in serbatoi ripiegati
per nutrire un mese di fioritura
in primavera. La gioia è incessante,
effimera: spettacolo notturno
di luminosità, svanito
nel caldo sole del giorno dopo.
A questo serve anche la più breve succulenza.

[1]cactus tipico del deserto dell'Arizona.
[2]*gilded flicker* e *gila woodpecker* sono due uccelli tipici della zona che albergano in buchi scavati nel tronco del saguaro cactus.

SUDDEN GRACE

Stripped to the waist
and barefoot, I step on
matted marsh grass,
mounds of seaweed,
layered mussel shells.
How like a dream!
I drink blue heron,
a fine line sketched
against sky, its
guttural cry almost
a growl, inches above
water, now bluer
in the rising.

GRAZIA IMPROVVISA

Spogliata fino alla vita
e scalza, cammino su
cespugli di erba marina,
alghe ammucchiate,
gusci di mitilo a strati.
Quale sogno!
Mi colmo di airone blu,
una sottile linea tracciata
contro il cielo, il suo
richiamo gutturale quasi
un ringhiare, appena
sopra l'acqua, ancora più blu
nel salire.

PILGRIMAGE TO THE
BLACK VIRGIN OF MONTSERRAT

After Dorothy Giles

Past fold on fold of purple,
we climb the holy mountain

majestic, rising above lesser
green-clad hills, impregnable in greenness.

In a deep cleft below coursed turbulence,
caves inaccessible as the Holy Grail.

Up sheer rock, the gorge,
and beyond, a blur.

Time's giant fingers
cleave the peak.

PELLEGRINAGGIO ALLA
VERGINE NERA DI MONTSERRAT

Secondo Dorothy Giles

Superando piega su piega di porpora
scaliamo il monte sacro

maestoso, lasciando sotto di noi le colline
verdeggianti, insuperabilmente verdi.

In un profondo crepaccio sotto corsi turbolenti
grotte inaccessibili quanto il Sacro Graal.

Al di sopra pura roccia, la gola,
e oltre, l'indistinto.

Le dita gigantesche del tempo
solcano la cima.

IV. Coagulatio

THE HUM

Water pours off the gutterless roof.
A squirrel defies gravity. Through
branches, the interminable sky.
Past thirteen curtainless windows,
I walk the room's perimeter,
poised in the wake of the first flash.

I'm talking about expectancy.

This night is marred by brooding,
desire. Lightning bathes the untilled
landscape, the ripening
mud, the only thing
that exists besides my body,
and your thoroughly examined heart.

IL VIBRARE

L'acqua scroscia dal tetto senza grondaia.
Uno scoiattolo sfida la gravità. Attraverso
i rami l'interminabile cielo.
Dietro tredici finestre senza tende
cammino lungo il perimetro della stanza,
sospesa nella scia del primo fulmine.

Parlo di aspettativa.

La notte è sciupata dal rimuginare,
dal desiderio. Un fulmine inonda il paesaggio
incolto, il maturare del
fango, l'unica cosa
che esiste a parte il mio corpo
ed il tuo cuore minuziosamente visitato.

American Visionary Art Museum

I.
I know why freak shows exist
Human Worm, Bearded Lady
to show me my shadow self,
aroused by crucifixion,
grotesque beneath the veneer.

II.
Schizophrenia in verdant relief—
bloomers, intricately stitched,
displayed under glass—
had she known,
would she have labored
frenetic for beauty,
or worn them threadbare?

III.
Inside the burning house,
a woman trapped, seething,
prayed for escape
from senseless cremation.
And God said: *Paint doors.*

MUSEO AMERICANO DI ARTE IRREALE

I.
So perché esistono certi spettacoli ripugnanti,
Verme Umano, Donna Barbuta,
per mostrarmi il mio aspetto ombra
suscitato da tormento,
il grottesco sotto l'apparenza.

II.
Schizofrenia in rilievo verdeggiante—
calzoncini intricatamene ricamati,
esposti sotto vetro—
se lo avesse saputo,
avrebbe faticato
freneticamente per bellezza
o li avrebbe portati logori?

III.
All'interno della casa in fiamme
una donna intrappolata, bruciando,
pregò per sfuggire
da cremazione senza senso.
E Dio disse: *Dipingi porte.*

WOMEN IN A HOT TUB

We climb in
    one
       by
          one,
heeding the proximity
of one another's skin:
the statuesque,
the hour-glass missing a breast,
the tanned, buffed, pedicured-perfect,
the childless one with her palpable womb,
the langorous, the sensual
one filling space for two,
the runner with muscled sighs,
and I, wet beneath
my nostrils. Everything
smells like sex.

DONNE IN UNA JACUZZI

Entriamo
    una
        per
            volta,
attente alla prossimità
una alla pelle dell'altra:
la ben proporzionata,
la clessidra con un seno mancante,
l'abbronzata, lucidata, perfetta di pedicure,
quella senza figli con la pancia palpabile,
la languida, la sensuale
che occupa spazio per due,
la sportiva con sospiri muscolosi,
ed io, bagnata sotto
le narici. Ogni cosa
odora di sesso.

POEM FOR JACK SPICER, DEADBEAT POET

You never found the perfect partner,
that mute, nubile eunuch
with mirrors for eyes.

So you neglected your bitter body,
perspired beer and cheap brandy,
your fingers marred by Kool stains

and truths
        and lies
                and half-truths.

You held court in Aquatic Park,
your calloused radio tuned to
the ball game. Your cup filled up,

with venom
        and hurt
                and fruitless pursuits,

incessant, inexplicable couplings—
men, women, boys—and then
your cocksure rivalries

with the likes of Ginsburg, Persky,
Duncan, Ferlinghetti. I could go on.
Shall I go on?

POESIA PER JACK SPICER, POETA SFINITO

Non trovasti mai il partner perfetto,
quel muto, nubile eunuco,
specchi al posto degli occhi.

Così trascuravi il tuo corpo amaro,
sudavi birra e scadente brandy,
le tue dita rovinate da macchie di Kool[1]

e verità
    e bugie
        e mezze verità.

Tenesti corte nell'Aquatic Park,
la tua radio incallita sintonizzata
sul gioco del pallone. La tua tazza colma

di veleno
    e dolore
        e vane ricerche,

incessanti, inesplicabili accoppiamenti—
uomini, donne, ragazzi—e poi
le tue presuntuose rivalità

con i simili come Ginsburg, Persky,
Duncan, Ferlinghetti. Potrei continuare.
Devo continuare?

[1]Kool: sigarette fatte di tabacco e mentolo, particolarmente associate agli anni 60.

A Fine Narration

A girl with no tongue
wears a rope of scar at her throat.

On her grave, the roses will be hours—
pale, worn as a woman's coat.

She is feckless, that girl,
cheated of girlhood,

silenced, swallowing the father's
bile: all his losses, profane blades.

Shameless, she carries on,
finds her right place on water—

whales dive and rise in pairs, wave
flukes to greet the gannets, to drown

out weeping. They are whole.
They have lives of their own.

UN ECCELLENTE RACCONTO

Una ragazza senza lingua
porta un filo di cicatrici sul collo.

Sulla sua tomba, le rose saranno ore—
pallide, consumate come il soprabito d'una donna.

È inerte, questa ragazza,
defraudata dell'infanzia,

zittita, ingoiando la bile
del padre: tutte le sue perdite, lame profane.

Senza vergogna, prosegue,
trova il suo giusto posto sull'acqua—

balene si tuffano e risalgono in coppia, agitano
le code per salutare le sule[1], per sopprimere

le lacrime. Esse sono integre.
Hanno la loro propria vita.

[1]uccelli tuffatori (della famiglia dei pellicani) del Nord Atlantico.

V. MORTIFICATIO

DECONSTRUCTING SORROW

"Show me sorrow."
Everyone was eager.
A kind man offered Chinese characters—
Lid: a perpendicular stroke bissecting a parallel line
Mouth: four lines to make a square
Clothes: five sweeping strokes, for sleeves and dragging robes—
these she had tattooed
to her thigh
to remind herself:
Lid becomes covering.
Mouth and Clothes become
cry of mourning.
Everyone assured her
This was sorrow.

SMANTELLARE DOLORE

"Mostratemi dolore."
Tutti si proposero.
Un uomo gentile offrì caratteri cinesi—
Palpebra: un tratto perpendicolare, dividendo una linea parallela
Bocca: quattro linee che formano un quadrato
Vestiti: cinque ampi tratti per maniche ed abiti a strascico—
li aveva tatuati
sulla sua coscia
per ricordarsi:
Palpebra diventa copertura.
Bocca e Vestiti diventano
grido di dolore.
Tutti le assicuravano
Questo è dolore.

HOLD IT. WAIT.

I.
His eyelids!
Do they flicker?
There's a fresh cut
on his brow, from the fall.
His friend hands me
the Red Sox cap
he was wearing. This is
the night he died.

II.
Open mouth. My hand
goes up in terror.
Mouth an O grown
to fevered wailing,
to see his slack
jaw, lips pried wide
for tubes, the gravity
of his impotent heart.
Never *I love you*
from that mouth, that
broad set of lips that
smile, that snarl. Sing for me!

continued

FERMATI. ASPETTA.

I.
Le sue palpebre!
Tremano?
C'é un taglio fresco
sul sopracciglio, per la caduta.
Il suo amico mi porge
il berretto dei Red Sox
che portava. Questa è
la notte in cui morì.

II.
Bocca aperta. La mia mano
va su per il terrore.
La bocca una O divenuta
gemito febbrile
vedendo la mandibola
allentata, le labbra allargate
dai tubi, la gravità
del suo cuore impotente.
Mai *ti amo*
da questa bocca, queste
due labbra piene che
sorridono, che ringhiano. Canta per me!

continua

III.
I begin to wear his clothes.
Black jacket full of vice:
condoms, cigarillos,
scratch tickets.
Red sweater. Black
t-shirt. I prefer his clothes.
I wear his pants—
green cords. Our legs
the same lean stretch.
He was a long drink
of the sweetest waters.
All mine, the smell of him.
I should have known
it wouldn't last.

III.
Inizio a portare i suoi vestiti.
Giacca nera piena di vizi:
preservativi, cigarillos,
biglietti 'gratta e vinci'.
Maglione rosso. Maglietta
nera. Preferisco I suoi vestiti.
Indosso I suoi pantaloni—
velluto verde. Le nostre gambe,
stessa magra lunghezza.
Era un long drink
delle più dolci acque.
Tutto mio, l'odore suo.
Avrei dovuto sapere che
non poteva durare.

PINS AND ROSES

The dream is filled with the heads of roses,
scattered across a table, spilling
onto the floor, they mark a path to goats

who screech and bray and go silent, throats sliced.
A man is chained by his feet from the ceiling.
His blood falls like rain, a liquid ribbon streaming.

I turn to roses: hundreds of ruined beauties,
each stabbed at the stigma by a sharp silver pin.
Thoughts of flowers go deeper than looking.[1]
Life is like that. Death too. And love.

[1]Title of 1993 art installation by Chen Hui-chiao.

SPILLI E ROSE

Il sogno è pieno di corolle di rose
sparse su un tavolo, cadendo
per terra indicano un sentiero a capre

che stridono e sbraitano e tacciono, gole tagliate.
Un uomo appeso dal soffitto, piedi incatenati.
Il suo sangue cade come pioggia, un nastro liquido che scorre.

Divento le rose: centinaia di bellezze rovinate,
ognuna trafitta nello stigma da uno spillo d'argento.
Pensieri di fiori vanno più in profondità di uno sguardo.[1]
La vita è così. La morte pure. E l'amore.

[1]Titolo di un'istallazione d'arte di Chen Hui-chiao, 1993.

THE DIFFERENCE

I wrestled your ashes from the funeral urn,
a cylinder, too narrow at the neck. The plastic bag
held fine sand, a crumbled wall of ecru and pearl.
I tried to weigh you on the bathroom scale.
I held you, stepped on the scale, stepped off,
put you on the edge of the sink, stepped on again—
holding, not holding: the difference.
I didn't trust it. I took your ashes to the market,
placed the bag on the produce scale,
watched it sway. I bought three nectarines,
each one unblemished gold, and crimson.
Six-and-three-quarter pounds
you weighed, two pounds less than at birth.

LA DIFFERENZA

Ricavai a stento le tue ceneri dall'urna,
un cilindro, troppo stretto al collo. La busta di plastica
conteneva sabbia fine, un muro crollato di écru e perla.
Tentai di pesarti sulla bilancia del bagno.
Ti tenni, salii sulla bilancia, scesi,
ti misi sul bordo del lavandino, risalii—
tenendo, non tenendo: la differenza.
Non mi fidai. Portai le tue ceneri al mercato,
posai la busta sul piatto della bilancia,
osservai l'oscillazione. Comprai tre nettarini,
ciascuno oro senza macchie e rosso cremisi.
Sei libbra e tre quarti
pesasti, due libbra meno che alla nascita.

AIRBORNE

We drove to the airfield. The ground crew
guided three planes out. We chose 756 QK,
snapped pictures of each other smiling on the runway,
ashes in our hands. The pilot readied for take-off.

I didn't go. I didn't want to go.

I watched them board, set up a beach chair outside
the gate, checked the time: 3:50 p.m.
After, my daughter climbed from the plane,
brushed empty hands against her jeans,
releasing the sorry plight of her brother,
my firstborn, into clear, sun-filled air.

IN VOLO

Andammo al campo dell'aeroporto. L'equipaggio di terra
portò fuori tre aerei. Scegliemmo il 756 QK,
ci scattavamo delle foto sulla pista, sorridendo,
le ceneri nelle nostre mani. Il pilota preparò il decollo.

Non ci venni. Non ci volevo andare.

Li guardai salire a bordo, misi una sdraia fuori
dal cancello, controllai l'ora: 15.50.
Dopo, mia figlia scese dall'aereo,
strofinò le mani vuote sui jeans,
liberando il triste destino del fratello,
mio primogenito, nell'aria limpida, permeata di sole.

THE GRAVE OF E. E. CUMMINGS

Nothing earthly matters once we're dead.
The man driving the cemetery truck says
he doesn't know where anyone's grave is.
I walk the sculpture path:
   Mirrors at my feet serve forest to sky.
   A broom rests on the step, against forgetting.
   Boughs of copper beech sweep the poet's chair.
Drenched in thirst, I find his modest stone
flush to the soil, lost in the shadow of CLARKE.
I kneel to clear away the crabgrass, to read the epitaph—
the years of his birth and death, 1894–1962,
and in all capital letters
EDWARD ESTLIN CUMMINGS
And death i think is no parenthesis[1]

[1]From *since feeling is first* by e.e. cummings

LA TOMBA DI E. E. CUMMINGS

Le cose terrene non importano più, una volta morti.
L'uomo che guida il carro del cimitero dice
di non sapere dove sono le varie tombe.
Cammino lungo il sentiero delle sculture:
    Specchi ai miei piedi offrono la foresta al cielo.
    Una scopa poggia sul gradino, per non dimenticare.
    Rami di faggio rosso spazzano la sedia del poeta.
Fradicia di sete, trovo la modesta lapide
a livello del suolo, persa nell'ombra di CLARKE.
M'inginocchio per togliere l'erba sanguinella, per leggere
    l'iscrizione—
gli anni di nascita e di morte, 1894–1962,
e, tutto in lettere maiuscole,
EDWARD ESTLIN CUMMINGS
E, penso, la morte non è una parentesi[1]

---

[1]Da *since feeling is first* di e.e. cummings

VI. Transmutatio

ALCHEMY

Where better than here
to come clean?
Far from my usual moorings,
I climb a labyrinth of fog:
a muslin shroud, lighthouse
unrelenting upon the cliffs.
Three horses appear, hovering
beside a fort of cannons
aimed at the sea where
rocks drown in iridescence,
and a humpback breaches,
the fin, quicksilver,
turning her into
the deep terminal dive.

ALCHIMIA

Quale luogo migliore se non questo
per chiarirsi?
Distante dai miei ormeggi soliti,
salgo un labirinto di nebbia:
un manto di mussola, un inesorabile
faro sulle scogliere.
Tre cavalli appaiono, sospesi
accanto ad una fortezza con i cannoni
che puntano sul mare dove
le rocce annegano nell'iridescenza
e una balena balza fuori,
la pinna, come mercurio,
spinge nella
profonda immersione finale.

AUBADE

Among tumbled sea glass,
white-winged bones of cod,
pollen of spruce on water,
a man climbs into his dory,
rows out, abandons his oars.
He smokes a cigarette, scans
the shore. From beside
the red-tinged pier,
I watch first light release
like dahlias, inviolate,
in the soft mons of moss.

On the hill, a house leans
into light. From its chimney
a gull summons impatience,
my wanderlust. In a stand
of wind-tossed trees, between
planks of the pier, in flesh
of hard-shelled mussels,
your tenderness
distant, amber.

AUBADE

Tra il vetro levigato dal mare,
le bianche ossa alate di merluzzo,
polline di abete sull'acqua,
un uomo sale nella sua barca,
s'allontana, poi lascia i remi.
Fuma una sigaretta, scruta
la riva. Dal vicino
molo dipinto di rosso
guardo la prima luce sollevarsi
come dalie, inviolate,
nei morbidi cuscinetti di muschio.

Sulla collina, una casa si protende
nella luce. Dal suo camino
un gabbiano richiama l'impazienza,
la mia voglia di viaggiare. In un boschetto
di alberi scossi dal vento, tra
i tavoloni del molo, il guscio duro
delle cozze e nella loro carne
la tua tenerezza
distante, ambrata.

FROGS

Hundreds of them
the source of sound, risen
from the bottom of the pond.
We breathe quietly so as
not to disturb them.
You lean against a large
moss-covered rock.
I want to take you right there
against that rock
and again around the bend,
in a sun-filled clearing,
against a tree, on the
leaf laden, God laden
path, on papery birch bark,
in the mud puddle, on that
patch of melting snow.
Take or be taken.
I want to bare myself
for your pleasure. Listen,
the water comes to life! The frogs
are yearning, legs spread behind them,
their eyes just above the water.

RANE

Centinaia
la fonte del suono, che sale
dal fondo dello stagno.
Respiriamo piano come per
non disturbare.
Ti appoggi ad una grande
roccia coperta di muschio.
Vorrei prenderti proprio lì,
contro quella roccia,
ed ancora dopo la curva
in una radura piena di sole,
contro un albero, sul sentiero
carico di foglie, carico di Dio,
sulla corteccia, come carta, delle betulle,
nella pozzanghera fangosa, su quella
chiazza di neve che si scioglie.
Prendere o essere presa.
Vorrei denudarmi
per tuo piacere. Ascolta,
l'acqua prende vita! Le rane
bramano, le zampe dietro allungate,
i loro occhi appena sopra l'acqua.

REDEMPTION

How to decipher the astonishing sky!
Tonight the lighthouse signals
a call. I take off my boots, roll up pants
to my knees, step into the frigid water.
A beacon flashes, another flickers.
I wade and wade and wonder,
Should I keep walking?
The water, eerily black, swirls
like blown glass. What love holds fast
vast oceans to this planet hurtling?

Kittiwakes circle above schools of capelin
hungry for shore, born to spawn there.
They are swimming the swim
of death through the bay. Grateful
they feed on the edges of all space,
heed the constant force, a dark energy.

REDENZIONE

Come decifrare il cielo meraviglioso!
Stasera, i segnali del faro
sono un richiamo. Tolgo gli stivali, arrotolo i pantaloni
fino ai ginocchi, entro nell'acqua gelida.
Un faro lampeggia, l'altro trema.
Guado e guado e mi domando,
Dovrei continuare a camminare?
L'acqua, paurosamente nera, crea un vortice
come vetro soffiato. Quale amore stringe
vasti oceani a questo pianeta che si affretta?

Gabbiani volteggiano sopra branchi di pesci cappellani
avidi della riva, nati per deporre le uova qui.
Nuotano il percorso
della morte attraverso la baia. Grati
si nutrono al limitare dello spazio,
ascoltando la forza costante, un'energia scura.

SOJOURN

Until now I did not know the gall and splendor
      of crows.
On the beach I find the foot of a bird,
carry it to my room, place it on the mantel,
      an immigrant fumbling.
I finger bones, stones, shells, shards, the severed foot,
      curled claws luminous,
all that I'll give back
to this ocean that takes my sorrow in its hold.

SOGGIORNO

Fino ad ora non sapevo della sfacciataggine e dello splendore
    dei corvi.
Sulla spiaggia trovo una zampa d'uccello,
la porto nella mia stanza, la poggio sulla mensola del camino,
    un immigrante goffo.
Tocco ossa, pietre, conchiglie, cocci, la zampa staccata,
    luminosi artigli arricciati,
tutto questo renderò
a questo oceano che possiede il mio dolore.

THE HIGHEST PLACES

Downy,
the hip-high heads of dandelions
nod at the field of lady's thumbs
that lead to a barn on the bluff.
Above and below, the blue
of Newfoundland
water, sky, lupine,
forget-me-nots,
my son's eyes.
Scaffolding is in place
for this foreshortened season.
The island's seabound mountains
feed on rolling capelin,
black and thick as oil slicks.
Tourists flock to villages
that list on the brink of grief
worn inside out, bound to pride,
a codless ocean, ghosts of the past
and missing. And still,
crows measure the perimeter of bays,
spread seed across fields and cliffs.
They nest in the highest places where
God's breath condenses into fog.

I Luoghi più Alti

Soffici,
le corolle dei denti di leone, alti fino ai fianchi,
annuiscono alle salcerelle sul campo
che porta ad un fienile sulla scogliera.
Sopra e sotto, il blu
di Terranova
acqua, cielo, lupini,
nontiscordardimé,
gli occhi di mio figlio.
L'impalcatura è al suo posto
per questa stagione accorciata.
Le montagne di questa isola, protese verso il mare,
si nutrono degli ondeggianti pesci cappellani,
neri e grossi come chiazze d'olio.
Turisti affollano i paesini
in bilico sull'orlo del dolore
portato al rovescio, esternato con orgoglio,
un oceano senza merluzzi, spiriti del passato,
mancanti. Ed ancora,
corvi misurano il perimetro delle baie,
spargono semi sui campi e sugli scogli.
Nidificano nei luoghi più alti dove
il respiro di Dio si condensa in nebbia.

ABOUT THE AUTHOR

EMILY FERRARA is an assistant professor of family medicine and community health at University of Massachusetts Medical School, where she teaches creative writing and communication skills. Her poems have appeared in *Lumina, The Worcester Review, Family Medicine,* and *Ballard Street Poetry Journal,* among others. A member of "Poem Works: Workshop for Publishing Poets," she has received recognition for her poetry from the Society of Teachers of Family Medicine in 2005 and the Worcester County Poetry Association in 2006. *The Alchemy of Grief* is her first full-length book. She holds a BS in Communications from Boston University, and an MA in Interdisciplinary Studies from Lesley University. Born and raised in Bridgeport, Connecticut, Ferrara resides in Worcester, Massachusetts, with her life partner M. Lara Hoke, and her daughter Deva Jasheway.

ABOUT THE TRANSLATOR

SABINE PASCARELLI grew up in Germany where she earned a degree in German language and literature at Dortmund University. She authors literature for children; her most recent book, published in Germany, is *Glenscheck & Co.* She has won fiction awards, from La Spezia, Italy and most recently, Mirabilia, in 2006. She has published her poems in various anthologies in both English and Italian, in *Only the Sea Keeps* for Bayeux Editions and in *Il Litorale, Città di Salò,* and *Pensieri di Donne.* Her poems have recently appeared in *Arabesques Review* (2007). She works as a translator of English, Italian, and German; many of her translations have been published by Italian publishing houses. Pascarelli lives in Tuscany with her husband Salvatore and their two sons, Marco and Claudio.

THE BORDIGHERA POETRY PRIZE

Announcing an Annual Book Publication Poetry Prize

Sponsored by
THE SONIA RAIZISS-GIOP CHARITABLE FOUNDATION
Offering a $2,000 Prize to an
American Poet of Italian Descent

GUIDELINES FOR COMPETITION

• *The prize, consisting of book publication in bilingual edition by Bordighera, Inc., is dedicated to finding the best manuscripts of poetry in English by an American poet of Italian descent, to be translated upon selection by the judges into quality translations of modern Italian for the benefit of American poets of Italian ancestry and the preservation of the Italian language. Each winning manuscript will be awarded a cash prize of $1,000 to the winning poet and $1,000 for a commis - sioned translator.* The poet must be a US citizen, but the translator may be an Italian native speaker, not necessarily a US citizen. The poet may translate his/ her own work if bilingually qualified. *Submission may be made in English only or bilingually.*

• The poet must submit **TWO** *copies of 10 sample pages of poetry in English on any theme.* Quality poetry in any style is sought. Universal themes are welcome. The final book manuscript length should not exceed 48 pages since, including the translations, the published, bilingual book will be 96 pages in length. To give the translator time to complete the work, the entire winning manuscript will not be due for at least 6 months after selection of the winner.

• The 10 sample pages of poems in English IN DUPLICATE should be on white 8 1/2 by 11 standard paper, clearly typed and photocopied. (Single spaced except between stanzas with no more than one poem to a page, though a poem may run on to more than one page.) Be sure to label all pages with titles of poems and number them from 1 to 10. *The applicant's name should NOT appear on any poetry pages.* Staple the pages securely together and *attach a cover page to each of the two copies with name, address, telephone, e-mail if applicable, and brief biograph - ical note of the author. The remainder of the manuscript should be anonymous.* Poems contained in the submission may have appeared in literary magazines, journals, anthologies, or chapbooks. Include an acknowledgments page if applicable.

THE BORDIGHERA POETRY PRIZE

GUIDELINES FOR COMPETITION
(continued)

• *If poems have already been translated into modern Italian, submission of a bilingual sample is encouraged* making a 20 page sample with a translation page following each English page. Include name and biographical note of translator on the cover pages.

• *Manuscripts will be judged anonymously.* The distinguished judge for the 2007 and 2008 awards is **Michael Palma.**

• Applicants should retain copies of their submission, which will not be returned.

• *Submissions must be postmarked by May 31st each year.* **Mail to:**

Founder: Alfredo de Palchi
Bordighera Poetry Prize
PO Box 1374
Lafayette, IN 47902–1374

• Include a *self-addressed stamped business-sized envelope* for notification of the winners.

• For acknowledgment of receipt, send a *self-addressed postcard.*

• The decision of the judges will be final. Winners will be announced by November each year.

• Bordighera, Inc. and the judges reserve the right not to award a prize within a given year if no manuscripts are found to be eligible for publication.

• The author and translator will share in the royalties in the usual amount of a standard book contract to be drawn between Bordighera, Inc. and the author and translator.

Printed in the United States
208733BV00003B/4-15/A

9 781884 419898